History of Hawai'i

THIS EDITION
Editorial Management by Oriel Square
Produced for DK by WonderLab Group LLC
Jennifer Emmett, Erica Green, Kate Hale, *Founders*

Editor Maya Myers; **Photography Editor** Nicole DiMella; **Managing Editor** Rachel Houghton;
Designers Project Design Company; **Researcher** Michelle Harris;
Copy Editor Lori Merritt; **Indexer** Connie Binder; **Proofreader** Susan K. Hom;
Authenticity Readers Dr. Naomi R. Caldwell, Kale Kanaeholo; **Series Reading Specialist** Dr. Jennifer Albro

First American Edition, 2024
Published in the United States by DK Publishing, a division of Penguin Random House LLC
1745 Broadway, 20th Floor, New York, NY 10019

Copyright © 2024 Dorling Kindersley Limited
24 25 26 27 10 9 8 7 6 5 4 3
004-339785-Jun/2024

All rights reserved.
Without limiting the rights under the copyright reserved above, no part of this publication may be reproduced, stored in or introduced into a retrieval system, or transmitted, in any form, or by any means (electronic, mechanical, photocopying, recording, or otherwise), without the prior written permission of the copyright owner. Published in Great Britain by Dorling Kindersley Limited

A catalog record for this book is available from the Library of Congress.
HC ISBN: 978-0-7440-9444-2
PB ISBN: 978-0-7440-9443-5

DK books are available at special discounts when purchased in bulk for
sales promotions, premiums, fund-raising, or educational use. For details, contact:
DK Publishing Special Markets, 1745 Broadway, 20th Floor, New York, NY 10019
SpecialSales@dk.com

Printed and bound in China

Super Readers Lexile® levels 310L to 490L Lexile® is the registered trademark of MetaMetrics, Inc.
Copyright © 2023 MetaMetrics, Inc. All rights reserved.

The publisher would like to thank the following for their kind permission to reproduce their images:
a=above; c=center; b=below; l=left; r=right; t=top; b/g=background
Alamy Stock Photo: Yvette Cardozo 28b, Danita Delimont, Agent / Dave Bartruff 3, Design Pics Inc / Hawaiian Legacy Archive / Pacific Stock 19t, North Wind Picture Archives 25bl, The Picture Art Collection 18br, Marlon Trottmann 12br, Chester Voyage 1, Zuma Press, Inc. 10–11, 30cl; **Bishop Museum Archives:** 19cra, 30tl;
Bridgeman Images: Christie's Images 12bl; **Dreamstime.com:** Evan Austen 22–23, Bennymarty 8–9, Innaastakhova 23crb, Rico Leffanta 16–17, Rainer Lesniewski 8b, Martinmark 4–5, Grondin Franck Olivier 23clb, Joey Swart 23bc, Juergen Wallstabe 14b, Wirestock 7tr; **Getty Images:** AFP / Mandel Ngan 27tr, Moment / Nisa and Ulli Maier Photography 6–7, 30bl, Jim Sugar 9br, Universal Images Group Editorial / Pictures from History 21tr;
Getty Images / iStock: Daniel Bendjy 29tr, E+ / Fat Camera 29tl, 30cla, Steven Gaertner 20b;
Hawaii State Archives: 24tl, 25br; **Library of Congress, Washington, D.C.:** LC-DIG-stereo-1s12105 / Pretty hula dancing girls with wreaths of flowers, Honolulu, Hawaii. Hawaii Honolulu, 1923. Photograph.
https://www.loc.gov/item/2018647440/. 13t; **The 'Aha'ula Collections:** Brook Kapukuniahi Parker 15t;
The Honolulu Star-Advertiser: John C. Poole 20cr, 30cl

Cover images: *Front:* **Dreamstime.com:** Evgenii Naumov b; **Getty Images:** 500px / Warren Ishii; **Getty Images / iStock:** Nancy C. Ross r; *Back:* **Alamy Stock Photo:** NZ / BT cra; **Dreamstime.com:** Evgenii Naumov clb

All other images © Dorling Kindersley Limited

www.dk.com

This book was made with Forest Stewardship Council™ certified paper – one small step in DK's commitment to a sustainable future. Learn more at www.dk.com/uk/information/sustainability

Level 1

History of Hawai'i

Libby Romero

Contents

6	What Is Hawai´i?
10	The First Hawaiians
14	Royal History
20	Time of Change

26 Hawai´i Today
30 Glossary
31 Index
32 Quiz

What Is Hawai´i?

Hawai´i is many things.

It is a chain of islands in the Pacific Ocean.

It is home to Mauna Loa.

That is the largest active volcano on Earth.

Big-wave surfing started here.

And Hawai´i is the 50th state in the USA.

Mauna Loa

The Hawaiian Islands lie above a hot spot inside Earth.

The hot spot melts rock.

The melted rock rises to the surface.

It cools and hardens.
It makes islands.

The First Hawaiians

About 1,500 years ago, the first people came to Hawai´i.

They came from the Marquesas Islands—about 2,000 miles (3,219 km) away.

The people sailed across the ocean in big canoes.

They knew how ocean currents move.

They used the stars to find their way.

Early Hawaiians knew how to farm and fish.

They could carve, weave, and make medicines.

The people honored the land and the sea.

They also honored many gods and goddesses.

Kūkāʻilimoku, god of war

Pele, goddess of fire and volcanoes

The people had no written language.

They sang and chanted stories.

They performed hula, too. Hula dances told stories.

Royal History

Over time, more people sailed to the islands.

The people divided the land into regions.

They divided themselves into groups.

Group leaders were called Ali´i [uh-LEE-ee].

They were the chiefs.

The chiefs ruled the regions. But they wanted more power. They fought to control land.

One chief wanted to unite the people of the islands.

His name was Kamehameha [kuh-may-huh-MAY-uh].

Kamehameha battled the other chiefs.

He won.

In 1810, he became Hawai´i's first king.

King Kamehameha I

Kamehameha ruled for nine years.

After he died, his oldest son became king.

Kamehameha II helped make a written language for his people.

When he died, his younger brother ruled.

Under Kamehameha III, Hawaiians learned to read their language.

King Kamehameha III

constitution

In 1840, Kamehameha III announced a new constitution.

He shared his power with the people.

Hawai´i became an independent kingdom.

Time of Change

People from other places heard about Hawai´i.

They saw opportunity.

So, people flocked to live on the islands.

And Hawai´i began to change.

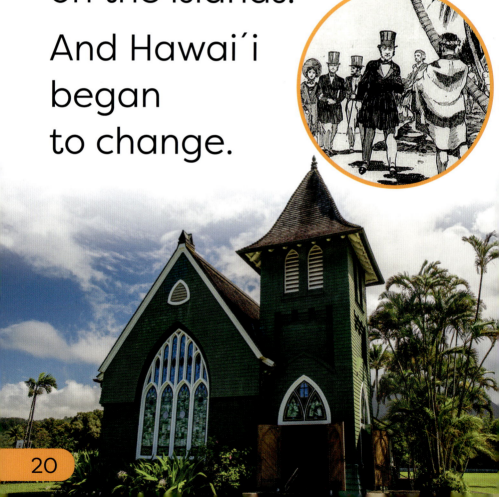

Captain James Cook

Captain James Cook was the first European to set foot on the islands.

He sailed there in 1778.

In 1820, American missionaries arrived.

They built churches.

They preached against Native Hawaiian beliefs and traditions.

Hawaiian culture began to fade away.

Newcomers bought land.

They cut down sandalwood trees. They sold the wood for a lot of money.

They planted large farms.

They grew sugarcane, coffee, and pineapple.

Workers came from all over the world.

Soon, there were more newcomers than Native Hawaiians on the islands.

King Kalākaua

In 1887, wealthy landowners forced King Kalākaua [kah-LAH-kao-ah] to sign a new constitution.

It took power away from Native Hawaiians.

It gave power to foreign landowners.

Liliʻuokalani [lee-LEE-ooh-oh-kah-lah-nee] was Hawaiʻi's last queen.

She tried to give power back to the people.

But rich Americans took over the government.

In 1900, Hawai´i became a US territory.

In 1959, it became a US state.

Queen Lili´uokalani

Hawai´i Today

Today, millions of people visit Hawai´i each year.

Visitors go to ´Iolani Palace.

That is where Hawai´i's kings and queens lived.

Visitors tour the capital, Honolulu.

Barack Obama was born there.

He was the 44th president of the USA.

Barack Obama

Only one in 10 people living in Hawai´i today is a Native Hawaiian.

But the Hawaiian culture is strong.

Children learn from their parents.

They surf along Hawai´i's shores.

They build canoes and perform hula.

Native Hawaiians celebrate traditions that started here long ago.

They share their culture with the world.

Glossary

constitution
a document containing the laws used to govern a nation

hula
a traditional Hawaiian dance

missionaries
people sent by a church to teach or convert others to their religion

current
the movement of a body of water in a certain direction

surfing
riding the ocean waves on a surfboard

Index

Ali'i 14

canoes 11, 29

chiefs 15, 16

constitution 19, 24

Cook, James 21

gods and goddesses 12

hot spot 8

hula 13, 29

Kalākaua, King 24

Kamehameha I, King 16, 18

Kamehameha II, King 18

Kamehameha III, King 18, 19

kings and queens 16, 18, 19, 24, 25, 26

Lili'uokalani, Queen 24, 25

Marquesas Islands 10

Mauna Loa 6, 7

missionaries 21

Obama, Barack 27

queens and kings 16, 18, 19, 24, 25, 26

surfing 6, 28

volcanoes 6, 12

Quiz

Answer the questions to see what you have learned. Check your answers with an adult.

1. How did ancient people first get to Hawai'i?

2. Which chief united the Hawaiian Islands?

3. Who was the first European to visit Hawai'i?

4. How did missionaries work to change Hawai'i?

5. Which US president was born in Hawai'i?

1. They sailed across the ocean in big canoes 2. Kamehameha I
3. Captain James Cook 4. They built churches and preached against Native Hawaiian beliefs and traditions
5. Barack Obama